A POET'S OUD

Poetry From My Heart

WAEL AL-SAYEGH

WRITERSWORLD

i

A POET'S OUD

Copyright 2006: Wael Al-Sayegh

ISBN 9948-03-272-1

Published by Wael Al-Sayegh in conjunction with Writersworld Limited

WRITERSWORLD
9 Manor Close
Enstone
Oxfordshire
OX7 4LU
England

Acknowledgments

To my mother, Khadijah Salem Al Arrayed for raising me up to be what I am. To my siblings, Amal, Mona, Reem & Hassan Al-Sayegh, for keeping me on my toes. To my wife Shamilla Jakoet, for saying yes and keeping me going even when I had given up. To Samineh Shaheem for her wisdom. To Hani Alaali, Rashid Abuhassan, Fareed F. Al Hinai, Hassan Al Redah and Waddah Ghanem for standing by my side when no one else did. To Geoff Thompson for being Geoff Thompson. To Deborah Brown and Mala Talwar for their reviews and comments. To the team at Writersworld Limited specifically Graham Cook for his wise council, Laurie McAdams for her honesty and Laura Booth for eloquence. Also, thanks must go to Anil Tejwani for his professionalism.

Cover Photograph: Courtesy of
www.droud.com

Dedicated to the loving memory of
Yumna Uthman Jakoet
1974- 2005

Index of poems

Poetry

It's the capturing of an essence;
It's the crystallization of a lesson;
It's a novel reduced to a page;
It's Wisdom dancing for you on a
golden stage.
Poetry is a symphony of the soul
and the conductor's baton is in your
hand.

It's a moment of inner peace,
a breath-taking view.
It's something that is truly understood
only by a few.
It's a lot of sleepless nights filled with
much frustration, anxiety & fear.
It's something I can read to myself
time and time again and still shed a
tear.

Poetry can be sad, happy, can make
you laugh or make you cry.

It's your chance to express yourself
without anyone asking you why.

It's a dance with your imagination, a
release from much pain,
or just something to help keep you
sane.

It's my island in the middle of a
stormy sea.

It's the only place I can truly be me.
But more importantly, it's a God given
gift to help me see
how worthy a subject I can be.

Poetry can be
a well tuned engine.
A perfect landing of a plane.
A Prostration to God you wish to
prolong.

It's the time you walked out of your comfortable but slow, self-murdering job and decided to live.
It's when you decided to stop taking, and learnt how to give.

It's the perfect execution of a movement you've spent a long time training.

It's the sound of your manuscript being dropped in the mail-box on its way to a potential publisher.

It's when the universe saved your life by giving you a sign.
It's when you and your wife climaxed at the same time.

Poems like these are the most beautiful of all. For the greatest poems in our lives are not those that are written, but those that are lived.

An Arabian Pearl Diver

In the days of old, Arabian pearl divers in
the Gulf had to leave their families to go
dive for pearls for five months of the year.
For five months they lived on the sea with
their loved ones nowhere near.

Our museums will tell you the story of the
pearl diver's life. The daily routines, the
sailor's songs, the equipment used, the
risks and the rewards. But no one has told
the world the story of the Arabian pearl
diver's passion. Guess the story must have
been waiting for me. For passion is
something I love to see.

Imagine, if you will, the passion a pearl
diver and his wife would have to produce
on the night of his departure. Imagine how
they would make love that night. That one
night must feed their souls for at least half
the year, maybe even a lifetime for neither
of the them knows, if they would ever
meet again. But the wise of all nations

have always said, that the presence of
death is what gives us true life.

Love your partner in such a way that even
when you are separated from each other
your pleasant memory never goes out of
fashion. That's the message behind the
story of the Arabian pearl diver's passion.

Three From Three

Angry eyes reflect nothing, but a soul that
is weak, and does nothing but despise.
Anger clouds one's vision like a storm
that blows one's ship far away from its set
mission.

Anger can turn a child's smile into an
insult and a threat. Anger will have you
blaming your own mama for loosing all
your money on that stupid bet.
But a life without anger would not
produce patience, for a patient human is
no stranger to anger.

Patience is feeling anger flow through
your veins and yet maintain peace from
within. It's having the urge to smash, kick
and scream, yet at the same time, being
able to tan your soul under love's beam.

The same holds true for bravery. Bravery
is not the absence of fear. It's moving
forward when the feeling of sheer terror is
near. Bravery is shitting yourself when

looking into your opponent's eyes. It's taking your opponent on despite their menacing size.

True friendship also follows the same formula. True friendship is not watching your friends' back whilst they are here. It's watching their backs when they are long gone and nowhere near.

I learnt the above whilst reflecting on the words of Imam Ali Bin Abi Taleb (AS), who said you will only acquire three after three occur, patience when anger stirs, bravery when fear sings you a song, and true friendship only when you are long gone.

Andalusia Nights

The Arabs entered Spain with love. They lived there with love, and they left with love too. It was a love relationship through and through. Spain and Arabia produced one of the best love stories history ever knew.

Many of the remains of this love story are still standing today. Go to the Al Hamrah Palace in Granada and see for yourself. Walk through the courtyards of love and feel the passion. It was courtship from first sight, not some fort erected in haste after some blood-drenched fight. I think Spain was Arabia's first true love. For only love can last that long. Hate in comparison to love is a very short song.

Do you remember your first true love? Or should I say "Why, do you still remember them even until today?" Many things in life may change and alter, but your first true love is never forgotten. Often remembered in a private smile as images of them are retrieved from our special moments' file.

My first true love was called Maria Lourdez. I called her Lula for short. We met at the university, under the dark grey clouds of Glasgow. Her Spanish temperament reminded me so much of home. Her skin was as mine, potentially dark in tone.

Whenever I went to visit my first true love, the sound of the Glasgow rain I had to walk through would turn into the rhythmic clapping of gypsy hands.

When together, we would feed each other's souls by living out our chosen dreams. She would sing and dance for me, and by so doing evoke a thousand and one poems in my hearts mind. I would then take what she had given me, and compose for her poetry. The Spanish Star and the Arabian Poet, sounds like a fairy tale don't you agree? Well, it was exactly that.

We were a dream to each other. An oasis of sanity in a world gone mad; and having to leave each other made us both very sad. But despite the years gone by, I have not forgotten her and so…

Let this very poem be my Al Hamrah Palace gift to her. Proof that one's first true love is not just in the past, but a monument that will forever last.

The Man Who Ate My Best Friend

I used to have a best friend who I
spoke to everyday. Shared my
thoughts and feelings with. A partner
in crime in every single way.

But then he got married and is now
holier than thou. Ridicules and looks
down upon others who do what we
once did.

He looks at those days of old with a
sense of shame.
A time he could have done without. I,
on the other hand, look at them with
pride. For they helped make me what I
am today.

We used to speak about what is truly
important. Now we speak of matters
that are not.

He has grown a huge belly, a distant
shadow of the slender man he once
was.

Alas, my friend is now long gone,
deep in the belly of the man I see
today.
But every now and then, my best
friend breaks free,
And blesses me with his presence.

When I see him I am reminded of how
much I truly miss him.
But then as quickly as he appears he
vanishes.
Back inside the belly of the man who
ate my best friend.

Gardening

My gardener decided to skip town, left
the garden helpless with no one
around.

The garden is small so I decided to roll
up my sleeves and tend to the garden
with care, for dying flowers were a
sight this poet could not bear.

The moment my fingers felt the earth,
an overwhelming feeling of joy came
to me. The gardener in me had
awoken.

All of a sudden I knew what this small
garden needed to grow.
It needed Love.

Slowly but surely, the flowers began to
grow.

Gardening really humbled me in many ways, literally brought me down to my knees, and this is me with just the flowers, imagine what I'll be like when I move on to the trees.

Nando's

"It is indeed an honor for a chicken to be a Nando's chicken," said the hen to her chicks.

"Always live your lives in a good manner. Eat only what is healthy. Sleep early and you must always never forget to share. After all, Good chickens go to Nando's, bad ones go elsewhere."

What I love most about Nando's is not the great tasting chicken, nor their famous Peri Peri sauce. What tickles my taste buds most is the fact that it's a story of a cultural fusion.

It's the goodness of Europe and Africa put on a platter. All grilled to perfection, so that you can't blame them for you getting any fatter.

You have to eat it with your bare
hands, bohemian style. Let that ancient
old sauce seep right through your
fingers. Close your eyes and let the
unique flavour linger.

It's Halal, wherever you go,
and their staff always put on a good
show.

It's healthy fast food that tastes great.
And I need not remind you that their
chips are not fried but baked.

You can eat it extra hot, hot, or if you
are like me, mild.
They will even have a colouring kit
ready for your child.

All the above are good reasons why
you should eat at Nando's.

But for me it's all the above plus one
more. One more reason why I would
never give Nando's a pass.

My wife's South African.you see and
if I did,
she'd kick my ass.

Eid Sandals

Just before the coming of Eid, I head to the marketplace to buy a new pair of sandals. I pass the area where they sell electronics, and the stall that sells all those bangles.

I get to the sandal rack and scan it from top to bottom. I see a pair I really like but realize my friend Waddah already has them. I continue to look for something that speaks to me, for price is no obstacle when it comes to my Eid sandals, you see.

I pick a nice pair, not too loud, nor too dull, and try them on. They fit me just fine; and for the price of 75 Dirhams, they could be mine. Now the latest fashion trend says for Eid Sandals, 75 Dirhams is too cheap, most have to spend at least 300 Dirhams to walk away feeling pretty neat.

I pick a few sandals at random just to compare the price: 300, 400 and 550 Dirham sandals, all of which I would class

as very ugly ones I would never buy. But
those are the very same pairs that make
the sales record reach an annual high.

I think nothing of my high taste but low
cost item, and proceed to the pay counter.
And then I spot the perfect pair, hiding
from the customers' stare.
I try them on, and boy do they look chic! I
walk up and down wearing them, and have
no doubt that they're exactly what I seek.

I take my chosen sandals to the till, and
the lady punches in the keys. She looks up
at me with a smile and says, "35 Dirham
please."

Why is what I like always so inexpensive?
What determines a price anyway? Is it
material cost, a name, a trend? When I buy
sandals, I buy exactly that, sandals, not a
name. An ugly sandal with a name is only
bought by the very vain.

But many things in life follow the same
pattern. It's often someone else telling us

it's pretty and worth the price, when deep
down inside us we think it's nowhere near
being nice. It makes no sense to be forced
to buy something that is truly ugly. It
matters not about the name, or the fact that
it was worn by those with fame.

You decide for yourself what's cool.
Don't be a part of someone else's
thoughtless fashion school. The same
applies when you buy a car, a house, a
tennis racket, a pen, or some candles.
Or, as in my case, a pair of 35 Dirham Eid
sandals.

Marriage On A Bad Day

One day a murderer, the other a murdered
victim.

When will this killing ever stop?
When will love reign? When will this
union again appear to be sane?

On nights such as these, the blue sheets of
our bed turn into the Atlantic Ocean. With
me on one coast, and my wife the other.

If you were to knock on my door on such
a day. A day of much collision.
I'd probably answer the door wearing a
military helmet, equipped with the latest
night vision.

Marriage On A Good Day

I wake up beside an angel every day.
I wake her up with a shower of little
kisses, and she greets me with a smile.
She asks me if I would like to have
something to eat?

I answer by saying, "If it is my soul that
needs feeding, then know that your
existence is the key, and if it is my heart
you refer to, then know that your smile
has already nourished me."

Our bed on such a night turns into a
platter, a platter of human spaghetti
cooked by passionate Italian hands.

And if you were to knock on my door on a
day such as this,
a day glorious beyond belief, you'd
probably find me wearing very little, but a
rose between my teeth.

Oud

"Why does a Oud have such a big hollow
back?" the Arab child asked his old
grandfather. The grandfather looked into
his grandchild's eyes, and fought back the
tears, and said;

"When a son grows up and leaves his
home, the father is often sad and left
alone. He knows his son must pave his
own way, but somehow he wishes he has
more of a say on how his son paves his
way.

Now the Oud is a father who got
abandoned by his son. Not even an Eid
card did the son send, not even a call to
say, "Hi dad, is all OK?"
It's the sound of a son's voice a father
longs for. It matters not what they say.

One day, the Oud felt extra lonely and
began to cry, thinking of his son and all
the lonely days gone by.

When the Oud stopped crying, it began to sing, in the hope something from somewhere would come and comfort him.

As his sad song traveled through the air, a crowd began to gather. Soon the Oud realized greater things than him had been abandoned.

From the gathered crowd that had now formed a crescent, Islam approached the Oud. It told him of the story of its abandonment, how its wonderful fruits had been left on the floor. Everything from tolerance, mercy to free-thinking. Is it any wonder its boat is now sinking?

Then World Peace arrived. Walking along with a limp and a black eye. Speechless. Its protest could only be heard in the sound of its great painful sigh.

Integrity and Modesty came along as a pair, saying the world had forgotten about them too. Many now look at them with shame, like they are some kind of a weird flu.

Thank You and Please dropped by and said, "Oh wise Oud, we so enjoyed your song; it reminded us of our golden days that are now long gone.

Love came running, and stumbled onto the floor crying, saying it had been dumped for hate. Why is mankind so eager to choose a life with such an ill fate?

Now as they all approached the singing Oud, they all became one, and entered the Oud's consoling sack. And that, my dear child, is why the Oud; has such a big hollow back."

Tourist

When a tourist comes to your city, and
you wish to show them around, take them
to where the beauty of the land and its
native people can be found.

Don't take them to the shopping malls,
clubs, pubs, or fancy restaurants. Take
them to the hills, the valleys, the parks, the
ocean and the mountains.

Take them to where they may drink from
the local peoples' fountain.

Tire Henna

As I polish you with my hands for the last
time, I notice the battle wounds that cover
your body. I gently caress them and
remember the many adventures we shared.

You opened a world to me that gave me
much knowledge and reflection. You were
the very first childhood dream of mine to
come true. Through you, and through you
alone, I realized that I had the power to
make my dreams come true.
Your red-coloured start button started
more than just your engine.

Although it pains my heart to let you go, I
truly must. For the very forces that
brought you into my life are now telling
me to let you go.

As I leave you in the cold show room,
sparkling as new as the day you came into
my life, I notice that on a part of your tire,
the very feet that carried me home on
nights I did not think I would see the light

of the day, was a trace of dirt that had
obviously come from when the careless
mechanic rolled you in.

I quickly rushed to my car and got the tire
polish spray. I carefully reHennaed your
feet, making sure it was even all around.

The shop keeper looked at me with a smile
and said
"You don't really want to sell it, do you?"

I reply with the Tire Henna in my hand
No, but I must.

Divorce

To my family and friends, and all those
who thought my marriage would never
last. To those who see me now lying flat
on my face bleeding.
To them I painfully say, "You were right,
and I was wrong."

To my Ex's family and friends, to all
those who met me, and took me in as one
of their own,
I say thank you for being so kind. Thank
you for everything you did, and I hope we
can still remain friends.

To my Ex, I say only this, your hate was
far stronger than my love, and for that I
apologize.

But given the choice, I would do it all over
again and not change one bit. For the
whole process taught me so much. Painful
as it may seem now, I know I will look
back at this with great pride, for I picked

my soul off the ground knowing I truly
tried.
There is no shame in such a loss, only
much gain.

Boys With Toys

Every Friday after mosque, we mount our
quads on our trailers and head out into the
desert. Like rain drops that trickle down
mountains, we come together into streams,
rivers and then end up at the sea. The
desert is an ancient ocean, didn't you
know?
Only difference is its movements are
rather slow.

We Quaders are the surfers of this slow
moving ocean. We surf the dunes'
crescents from angles that defy gravity.
It's almost like we are on some invisible
rail.
We twist and turn leaving sprays of sand
in the air behind us, as we move forward
on our trail.

People go quading for different reasons.
Some do it for the adrenaline rush, others
for mental relief.
Some do it for the company, and others
for the scenery.

Me, I do it to visit my ancient teacher. The
desert inspires me to think like all good
teachers should. I ponder about how the
ripples in the sand are just like those in the
sea. How huge dunes as big as mountains,
change and shift with the wind. Its sands
tell me a story each week, it invites me to
look around, and think about what kind of
life I should pursue and seek.

Never go out to the desert alone, for it can
be a treacherous place. Always have
someone with experience riding with you,
just in case.

The group I go out with is an interesting
lot. Let me introduce you to some of them;
there's the joker of the lot. A man with a
big smile who always makes us laugh.
He's kinda chubby, and at times rather
loony. His name is, Mohd. Faredooni.
Then there is the stunt man of the group,
Omar Sawan. He pulls off his best stunts
when tourists are near. They take pictures
of him, and some even clap and cheer.

Then there's the godfather himself, Abdul Baset Al Janahi. He rides a legendary tiger-striped Yamaha 450, and in an uphill race, you better brace yourself cause he moves very swiftly.

Last but not the least there's me.
I'm the one at the back of the group, because I'm just too slow. It's got nothing to do with my Honda 400, it's just that I'm in no rush, how else can I enjoy the show?

But do you know what the most poetic parts are for me? It's the special moments in between, when we stop to rest and talk. We turn off our engines, and listen to the silence of the desert. Free from any man-made noise.

It's then that a mystical transformation occurs, a transformation that turns us from being men into boys. Boys in school ask each other; "What class are you in? Where did you get that lunch box from?"

These are real questions that seek an enlightened truth. Grown-ups in the city ask questions that have nothing to do with the truth. They ask; "What sect does he follow?" "How much does he earn?" But in the desert, we return to being boys. We ask about where you got your exhaust from? And what modifications have you done to your engine?

Out here in the desert, we are not CEOs, staff, sunni, shia, locals or expats, we are just boys with toys. How I wish we could stay boys in the city too. Being a boy in the city is the best way to take the desert home with you.

So thank you dear ancient teacher for showing me the importance of being a boy, and thank you, my trustworthy Honda 400, for being my favorite toy.

Zayed

"Give me agriculture and I will give you
civilization in return,"
were amongst his many wise words.

It's as if he was asking humanity out loud,
"What good are your high rise towers,
your factories and space stations if they
are built on foundations that forget their
indebtedness to the earth.
A truly civilized society is one that
nurtures its final resting place, and never
forgets its true roots no matter how
wealthy or technological advanced it may
become."

His origin was the desert, and he carried
its ancient beauty close to his heart
wherever he went,
and shared it with the rest of the world.

His generosity was as vast as the desert
itself. Giving not only to his people, but to
all those in need found far and wide.

I loved the way he humbly sat
international delegates on the ground,
making the earth his throne. He gave the
phrase "down to earth" a whole new
dimension.

He brought desert wisdom to the political
arena, spoke in words that were simple
and plain. No twist and turns hid his
intentions. For when a person's intentions
are pure, what need does it have of twists
and turns?

He danced with his people at their
weddings.
Was never too far away to hear them call,
and always picked them up, with tender
loving hands, if they were to ever fall.

The images of him surrounded by smiling
children will eternally be imbedded in our
souls.
It's as if he spoke to them in their very
own language; a language full of smiles
and laughter, innocence, purity, endless
hope and dreams.

He spoke to adults in their language too.
Perhaps trying to remind them that they
too were children once.

When he passed away
all mankind, with all its different races,
religions and creeds shed tears of sadness.
The birds and the gazelles also wept and
mourned. The earth on the other hand
wept from happiness not sorrow, for a
precious part of it had returned home.

More than just the heart and soul of the
nation,
he was our Abraham Lincoln, Mahatma
Gandhi, Nelson Mandela and Winston
Churchill all wrapped into one.
All hail our father, HH Sheik Zayed bin
Sultan Al Nahyan,
the greatest Emarati to ever walk under
the sun.

The Dubai In You

What does Dubai mean to you?
What does Dubai represent? When you
think of my beloved city, what is the first
thing that comes to your mind? Now, you
must be honest with me. I am a Poet, the
truth is all I care to see.

*Oh, your city is so clean, peaceful, safe
and tolerant! It has good schools for the
kids, good weather all year round, fun,
plenty of sun, concerts, shopping malls ,
fancy car. And camping in the desert
under the many stars.*

Ok, that's all fine and good, and yes I'm
very flattered. But give me an answer that
I can't find in a tourist book. Come now,
don't let this poet go home sad. Give me
what I seek, even if it's just a peek.

*Ok, Mr. Poet. Traffic jams, endless road
works, bad drivers and locals not doing
anything all day and still getting paid
millions whilst they sit.*

That's better. But I know you can do
better than that.

*Money laundering, tax evasion and some
dodgy short-term business plot.*

Ahh! Now we're getting warmed up. But,
seriously, is that all you've got?

*Fine, Mr. Poet, you've asked for it. How
does down-town Bombay, Russian mafia,
unpaid labor workers and prostitution
sound to you? Are you happy now, Mr.
Poet, or have we made you sad?*

Why would I be sad at that? It is your
reality you see in all these things, not
mine. Dubai like any other free city on
earth is what you want it to be.

You really are the decider there, not me.
But for what it is worth, allow me to
answer the question of what Dubai means
to me.

Dubai to me is a story of man who made it
through, when all expected him not to.

Dubai's very name is proof of this fact.
Not many of you know this but it's true,
the word Dubai comes from the word
Daba, which means young locust. No one
dared live here, you see.
It was nothing but a locust-infested area,
from its land to its sea.

Then along came a great man with a
vision and said, "Build me a city in
Dubai." You can imagine how they all
laughed at us, "*Why bother!*" they said
with a great sigh, "*You are just Dubai,
where nothing but the locusts fly.*"

But the great man was not affected by
what they said, and ordered the building of
a trade centre and a port. *What's wrong
with you people? You must be of the crazy
sort. You are nothing but Dubai, and at
this rate, you might as well kiss all your
oil money goodbye.*"

and take a look at Dubai today. One drive up the Zayed Highway will show you how wrong they all were, and how great that man was. The trade center is now the shortest building on the block; its accomplishments separated the city from the rest of the flock. The port is now busy all year round; its performance internationally crowned.

How did all this happen? What is the source of this alchemy that turned a locust-infested land into a great economic boom? In four words, it was the Al Maktoums.

His Highness Sheikh Rashid bin Saeed Al Maktoum had the vision. His more than able sons took the vision and made it their collective mission.

What I love about our royal family is not their great leadership skills or many accomplishments alone. That's all said and done. What impresses me most about them is how human they are. They walk the streets alone and even drive themselves to work. Of all the world leaders, I see them to be the humblest I ever knew.

Sure, you had a lucky break, and had the right leaders to get the job done, but the bubble is sure to burst, then you will all return to your original state of thirst.

Whilst you wait for this bubble to burst, let me tell you what Dubai has done. It has put all its systems in place, and is now even investing abroad. It has planned the development of all its land and now has to build on the sea, so by the time the bubble bursts, we'll be chilling, drinking tea.

But look at what's happening in Dubai, you are losing all that culture. I mean, where is Dubai heading to?

You just don't get it, do you? That's because you don't want to. Dubai, my friend, is not just a city, it is an attitude. So instead of asking where is Dubai

heading to, ask, rather, where is the Dubai
in you?

Sun Kissed

Let the sun kiss your beautiful skin
Looking dark is not a sin.

Your desert beauty is natural and so it
should always be.

Let go of the powder that whitens your
face, for it prevents your inner shine
from glowing.

Go easy on the make up, for your
beauty is already complete. Why add
to perfection?

Know that there are many in the world
who spend good money to travel to
places that give them your colour
temporarily. And here you are trying
to get rid of what you permanently
have been given?

Let the sun kiss your beautiful skin,

looking dark is not a sin.

Rasha, The Stock Market Flower

In the Dubai stock market, in the middle
of the trading storm, lives a flower called
Rasha.

Money makes people go mad, and in no
place can this be seen better than on a
stock market trading floor. Where the
mightiest and the bravest can be seen
crying as they head to the front door.

Whenever I pass by, I see Rasha
surrounded by poisonous thorns, shouting
and screaming at her, venting the anger of
their losses. They snatch the paperwork
from her hands, and leave without even a
thank you or a goodbye.

But no matter how many poisonous
thorns surround this stock market flower,
she stands dignified and strong, as if
mystically protected by some angelic
song.

I hear her heart tell them, "You don't have to shout at me. Why can't you just say please?" But these people don't come from the land of please. Dear Rasha, they come from the land of prison with thrown away keys.

Bad Service

In Dubai, you can't walk into a
bookshop and ask questions like,
"What do you recommend? Or,
Which do you think is better?

The shop assistant just looks at you
and has nothing to say.
To them books are just like vegetables
in a market. Tell them which ones you
want and how much you need in
weight.

I once asked for a book by title, author
and ISBN number. The assistant shook
his head and said
"No sir, we don't have that."

After looking for it myself, I found it
on one of their shelves.
I went back to the assistant and put
the book on the counter and quoted
Khalil Gibran,

"Work is love made visible." He looked back at me, with a look of a man trying to remember something and said, "No sir, I don't think we have that either."

It's the same when it comes to buying a car, eating at a restaurant or booking a holiday.
The worst is when it comes to things like teachers and doctors.
That's when the damage caused is more than an inconvenience. It's a generation's worth of damage. The difference between life and death.

You business owners might think you are being smart by cutting down on costs by hiring such people, but they are also cutting down on your potential to grow.

You must hire people who love to do what they do.

Those people who do not need to be
told.
Pay them well and just sit back and
watch them take your business to a
new high.

Hire someone who will tell you you're
wrong,
Hire some one who will make your
team strong.
Business is a team game,
say all those great business men who
now enjoy fame.

But if you remain to be "Give it to the
lowest bidder" junkies,
you have no one to blame for not
growing. For when you pay peanuts,
you get monkeys.

Driving in DXB

Why do you all act insane?
Swerving from lane to lane like you're
driving in some PlayStation game.
I got news for you.
The laws of physics treats us all the
same.

Ever seen what crushed metal can do
to a human body?
Ever had to see the remains of a loved
one after a road kill?
Trust me, it ain't no thrill.
Crushed metal knows not the
difference between a local and an
expat.
So why would you want to end up in
the Gulf News as a sad stat.

Know that when you drive you
represent not only you but your
people, your country, your religion and
your humanity.

Driving is not only a reflection of your manners, but also of where you got them from.

What I am saying here is not new.
So why do we still drive so bad?

Who do you blame?

The car manufacturers for building the cars to run so fast?
The parents for buying their young fast cars?
Or
The insurance companies for only insuring the car and not the driver?

Do you blame the constant road works and ever changing roads?
Or
A particular nationality or culture?
The driving instructors that need a few lessons themselves?
Or

The Dubai police for having laws they
don't really enforce?

Slow down man and stay with us for a
while.
Indicate when you're changing lanes.
I don't want to play, "Guess what I'm
going to do next" with you.
Courteously give way to others, wave
a "Thank You" and a "You're
Welcome" every now and then. And,
no, the service lane is not an extra lane
for you to take.

Stop flashing your lights behind me
trying to tell me to move. I like to
drive with peace in my heart, and your
flashing lights are seriously ruining my
well-maintained groove.

When that speed beeper goes off at
120KM, remember that that's your
parents calling, your children, your
wife, your friends and your life.

They're asking you,
Is it really worth it? Why not come
home late? Isn't that better than not
coming home at all?

So take heed of this poet's call;
Stop swerving from lane to lane like
your driving on some PlayStation
game.
And, remember, the laws of physics
treat us all the same.

The Magic Marker Man

Pick up an issue of Stuff, GQ or
Maxim from a Dubai magazine rack.
In between some of the pages, at times
the front cover even, you will see the
markings of the Magic Marker Man.

With a bold black marker pen he
scribbles out certain human body parts
so no one can see, but much to his
dismay, it's the parts that he has to
leave untouched that interest me.

The articles are left unmarked, even
though they are more graphic than the
images themselves, but the magic
marker man cannot read, and so does
not understand the nature of evil's
seed.

If safeguarding society from bad
influences is your mission, Mr. Magic
Marker Man, then I would suggest

you focus not on what the eyes can
see, but rather on how the mind reacts
to such images.

Your black coloured marker pen is not
big enough to cover the incoming
wave of information.
Try winning the battle from within
one's mind as opposed to the outside.
It's only there that you stand a chance.

The mind is where your arena is. It is
there that evil plants its seed.
So the first thing you should do is
learn to read.

New Locals

So you're a new local Emarati now?
No more shirts and ties for you.
Just overly starched, pure white,
Kandoorahs all the way through.

Now you get to talk down to others
and step on their feet. Just like they did
to you not so long ago. Your accent
has changed: more Bedouin-like
despite the fact you come from a
settlers' background. Your car
windows have suddenly become
tainted darker and you're so quick to
draw the "but I'm a local" or "this is
my country" line when things get
tough.

Don't worry, you're not alone.
The story is the same wherever you go.
The first generation nationalities in
most country are the ones that behave
the worst of all.

True locals tend not to advertise the fact that they are local.
They know what they are and no document can either give them that or take it away.

Their authenticity is not printed on a piece of paper, but marked on the ground,
with the blood their ancestors shed for the land.

Now before any of you old school locals start bragging, it is also important for you to know that true locals are not necessarily those who have been here the longest,
but rather those who have contributed to the country's growth the most.

Being a local is not a license for you to behave badly. If any thing, it's a duty for you to do good.

Mustang

Mustang is a Native American word for a
horse without an owner. A horse that runs
the great plains free, with nothing on its
back but the free spirit it is born with.

When the Native Americans first came
into contact with these *Drinkers of the
Wind*, they thought them as a gift sent
from above. To help them in their fight for
survival in a land that turned visitor into
settler, and settler into murderer and thief.
All for the price of a bottle of this or that,
agreed to by the big chief.

But the mustang gave Native Americans a
spiritual high like no other. They became
invincible warriors. For a mind that knows
not failure is a worthy adversary, even to a
fully armed cavalry.

Their adversaries were out-maneuvered by
a bunch of bareback riders. It was then
that a uniformed army general had an idea.

"Kill the mustangs. Kill the spirit and you
will kill the will." And so they did. With
the spirit now dead,
the mighty Native American warrior had
no choice but to eternally go to bed.

But a mighty spirit that fights and dies for
the legacy of the good never truly dies. It
simply transports itself into another
dimension. A dimension that allows it to
carry on its work, this time in peace. In the
peace it died to acquire, and sacrificed
everything for.
No Warrior of Light could possibly ask
for more.

The native UAE national and the Native
Americans are in many ways one.
Both are nomadic in origin, have vast
amounts of open land they call home.
They mainly marry within their tribes,
since they prefer their own home grown.
They both have seen their daily lives
rapidly changed, and both saw their
Chieftains make decisions that were very
strange.

They both depended on the existence of one particular animal for much of their daily keep, the Camel and the Buffalo gave them respectively much restful sleep. Both became minorities in their own countries. Their native tongue slowly replaced by another; and with it their ancestors' wisdom. Wisdom that took many years to accumulate is now at the mercy of destiny's fate.

Will we UAE Nationals ever be reduced to a tourist spectacle? Will we ever be asked to live on a reserve, an area where only locals reside? Perhaps we too have been abandoned by the tide.

My Fountain Pen

Just looking at you in this elevated state is
an inspiration to me. Just like the
mountains, the moon and the sea.

When I pick you up, time comes to a
standstill. When I draw you from your
sheath, the doors of eternity open, and the
most magnificent of human ceremonies
begin. It's when the angels of heaven
begin to sing.

No offence to any of you ballpoints or
typewriters out there, but nothing can
measure up to a fountain pen, not even the
latest PC. For you can't compare a plastic
plant found in the corner of an office
somewhere to a mighty oak tree.

I do not hold you too hard nor too gently.
This state of "in-between" forces me to
relax. As the blood circulation begins to
flow, my veins widen. My heart then
pumps my innermost thoughts and
emotions through my now expanded

veins, and through my finger tips they journey until they cascade down into the pond most call an empty page.

From my pond the thirsty may drink, the tired and weary may bathe, and the abused will be reminded that he/she is not a slave.

You turn my common blood from red to blue, you're the strongest weapon that mankind ever knew.
I adore the sound of you making love to paper.
I love watching your ink go from wet to dry.
You are indispensable to me, just like a sword to a Samurai.

Alone

Poets on the hunt for a poem must always hunt alone, even if they stand amongst many in a crowd. Their thoughts are somewhere else, in a place where only they must reside. These are the ancient rules of poetry, and all poets to this must abide.

Poets, must have the ability to detach themselves from reality. How else are they supposed to capture its essence?

Poets surf the waves of human thought and emotions. Share the thrill of the ride with all. They capture every moment like no other, including the fall.

This necessary, solitary requirement must be explained to the poet's loved ones. For it hurts them when they leave. But the hurt then will be ten times worse, if the very energy that makes up the poet is ceased.

One day a jealous wife asked her poet husband to choose her or poetry.

The Poet disappeared the next day leaving
behind his answer.

Would you prefer it if my love for you
slowly died day by day? Would you rather
not I leave, breathe and come back loving
you more?
Or would you rather I stay and watch the
miracle of our life turn into an unbearable
bore?
For the sake of our love, I would rather
spend my entire life alone, free, than
spend one minute with you in captivity.
You ask me to choose between you and my
poetry? I am my poetry. So what you're
actually asking me to do is to stop being
me.
My answer to that question is now in your
hands, for you and all to see.

Ying And Yang

I stand in front of a Ying and Yang poster.
I close my eyes and open my true poet's
eyes.
There I see Ying and Yang's true forms.
Two Siamese Chinese twins joined
together by the hip. They are like beautiful
Chinese dolls, dressed up in all their
ancient glory.
Looking at me with eyes that are dying to
tell their life's true story.

I smile at the sisters, and they at me, and
to each other we respectful bow. I look
into their souls and ask them one question,
"How? How do you wish to be seen, for
you are world famous now, perhaps the
most famous image that has ever been?"

"Yes, Mr. Poet, famous we are, but most
in understanding us, are very far.
To those who only see with their eyes, we
are decorative pieces of fun, something
cool or hip to put on the wall.

Something that will always sell in
peoples' stalls.

To others who think a little more, we are
examples of opposites, love and hate, cold
and hot, land and sea, war and peace. To
be, and not to be.

To those like you who feel us, we are not
two, but one. We are the blending of two
into one. We are one, Mr. Poet, only one.
Just like the creator of the sun.
Let us give you some examples. For we
know how poets love to sample.

We are Love. Love that has tasted the
rivers of hate.

We are Control. Control that understands
the power of fate.

We are Peace. Peace which knows the cost
of war.

We are Excitement. Excitement that has
experienced bore.

We are Death. Death that embraces the
presence of Life.

We are a Mistress. A mistress who is
loved like a wife.

We are Hunger. Hunger that has slept with
a stomach that is full.

We are sand paper. Sand paper that has
touched wool.

We are Freedom. Freedom that never
forgets the pain of slavery.

We are Cowardice. Cowardice that knows
the glory of bravery.

We would like to be seen as one. One, Mr.
Poet, one that is truly complete.
Not some poster that just looks pretty
neat."

Rosary

Thirty-three beads divided into three,
make up the Islamic design of a rosary.

What I marvel about rosaries are not
their wide variety of appearances, or
the precious stones they carry, or even
which hands the rosary chooses to
marry.

It's the thread that binds it all
together.

The single thread that is the backbone
of its existence. Without which the
rosary stones would scatter on the
floor. A rosary without a strong thread
is soon to be a rosary no more.

What is the single thread in your life
that, if cut, would cause you to be no
more? What pieces of you, if this

thread were cut, would lie scattered on
the floor?

My rosary thread is the heartfelt
existence of a just God. A God that
sorts the truth out and does not let it
fester, a God that deals in justice, in
this life and the next.

As for the pieces of me that would lie
scattered on the floor for all to see, it
would have to be none other than my
poetry.

Abra

One day a young businessman took an
Abra.

He paid the Abbar enough money to
have the whole Abra to himself.

As he was being carried from one side
of the creek to the other, he asked the
Abbar a question.

Old man, what do you know of the
science of investing?

Nothing, answered the Abbar.

Then half your life has passed you by,
no wonder you are just an Abbar.

Just then a series of huge waves from a
passing cargo boat bombarded the
small Abra.

The Abra began to sway and evidently was going to capsize.

The Abbar then asked the young businessman:

Young man, what do you know of the science of swimming?

Nothing, cried out the young man, as he held on to the Abra with all his might.

Then, my young man, all your life has passed you by.

Autumn And Spring

The desert is a land of extremes.
Everything from the intense moon, which
lights your soul, to the scorching sun's
beams.

The days are very hot, the nights very
cold. In it you are either a free human, or
one who is sold.

Summer and winter are the only seasons
you will find there. For the desert has no
in-betweens, no middle ground.

The same holds true for the people of the
desert. For people are a reflection of their
sands. Amongst them are the most read
and enlightened of humans, who will take
your challenge gracefully, on any
intellectually stage. But then you also
have those amongst them who still live in
the Dark Age.

They will either let you travel far and
wide, never standing between you and the

Maktoub destiny that you must chase, or they will be angry and jealous even of the wind that gently caresses your face.

Show them generosity and love, and they will offer you mercy, even after you have killed one of their own. But wrong them by taking their honor as fake, and they will make sure you and your offspring pay for the mistake.

When dealing with the desert people, you must understand the nature of their land. You must put yourself in their sandals.

At the same time, desert people who deal with city folk must also step into their shoes. They must learn to discover a middle ground, a place called the "in-between". There they will feel the other two seasons, of autumn and spring.

When?

When exactly do you last remember you
and your wife making the bed sing?
When precisely was it the gift of your
presence got replaced by buying her some
bling, bling?

When did you last wash your woman's
feet?
When do you last recollect pulling her up
a seat?

When was the last time you looked into
her eyes and said, "You are mighty,
mighty fine, and from the inner depth of
my heart and soul I say, I am truly
honoured to call you mine."

Passion when lost can always be regained;
you just have to acknowledge the fact that
passion has left the arena.
Then you must work on reconstructing
those special moments, and before you
know it, you will be docked back in
passion's marina.

Lee & Ali

Two men that are far more than they first appear to be, the legendary Bruce Lee and the eternal heavy weight champion of our hearts Mohammed Ali.

You can just look at pictures of these gentlemen in their prime and still be spell bound by what you see. Charisma exudes from them. Telling you tales of the endless possibilities human greatness can achieve.

Lee took the hidden beauties of his ancient culture and shared it with the rest of the world. He broke many sacred laws in order to do this, but how sacred is a law that prevents a human from growing? A criminal in an unjust system is a hero after all.

Like all good philosophers his words were very simple yet helped many accomplish many a complex task. Here is some of the wisdom he helped me gain:

All knowledge is ultimately self-knowledge. In your search for yourself you must have no boundaries, have no selected path, for once set in your way, you have trapped yourself in it. Use "No way as way and no limitation as limitation" as a motto to help remind you of your free state.

Acquire knowledge from wherever you can find it. Be colour blind in your search for yourself, only then can you truly see the meaning.

Now once you acquire the knowledge you seek, your task has not ended there. It just begins. For knowing is

not enough, you must apply. Willing is
not enough, you must do.
All this he taught us from the art of
Kung Fu.

Ali's biggest contribution to life was
what he did with his gloves off as
opposed to on. He took on the
strongest government of all and won.

He said I am not a slave to you or any
other man, for you will one day fall. I
am a slave to Allah, the mightiest and
greatest of them all.

As a poet his accomplishments are far
more than most will ever know.
He is author of the world's shortest
poem. Ask any real poet how
challenging writing short poems can
be. To capture a life-altering poem
using the least amount of words is
indeed no easy task. Many spend years
trying, but fail. So without further ado,

I present to you, the world's shortest
poem written by Mohammed Ali:

"Me, We."

I kid you not when I say I have read
400 page novels that have inspired me
less than these two words.

His skills as a poet do not end there.
For he now writes poems with no
words.
In my opinion, the highest level a poet
can ever attain in the art of poetry is to
reach this stage. It's where you and
your poems become one. It's when
your very silence is poetry.

Many of you mistake Ali today for a
man who's had something taken away.
I see him, as a man who has been
given the highest platform of honour.
That's what he meant when he wrote:
People often ask me questions I cannot

very well answer in words. And it makes me sad to think that they cannot understand the voice of my silence.

Both these great men uplifted their people, made them proud to be what they were, at a time when they saw themselves to be weak and ashamed. They taught them to be proud of where they came from and be proud to look the way they looked.

They both took their arts to levels of perfection. In the process became symbols of humanity. Their smiles lit up the souls of many across the globe. That is how I always remember them. Smiling.

Many people choose to see them differently than I do.
Some see a boxer, a martial artist, or an athlete.

Such people only see things with their
eyes. But in these two great human
beings, my heart will always see
The Philosopher and the Poet
Lee and Ali.

A Door Of All Seasons

"Why do you have a small door within
your door?"
Asked the little Gulf Arab girl to the
old wooden front door of her
recently deceased grandfather's house.

At first there was no reply, as it had to
wait for the mandatory silent period all
doors must adhere to before being able
to speak.

Usually people did not have the
patience to last through this initial
silence. Adults were particularly bad at
this and often left without getting an
answer to their questions.

The girl waited patiently for an
answer, as she looked at the old
wooden door with her large mascaraed
hazel eyes.

As the mandatory silent period passed,
a mystical gust of wind blew through
the small door causing her amazingly
thick black hair to sway in the air.
As the gust died down the old door
spoke.

"Back in my days, everything was
built to last.
Back then, your people were not as
rich as they are today and so were far
more practical and efficient with the
little things they had.
I was carved from such hands. Hands
that thought far ahead.

I am a door built for all seasons.
My small door is built for protection,
when enemy tribes attacked the city. I
once saved your grandfather's life by
forcing the attackers to squeeze into
the small door you see. This gave him
just enough time to escape by jumping
over the other side of the wall.

My small door also helps capture the cool breeze. It channels it into the courtyard and helps spread it to places it would not otherwise reach."

"So why have the big door then?" Asked the girl again.

My large door is built for generosity. When your grandfather got married, my larger door was opened wide to allow the maximum number of people in, to share in the joy and happiness that weddings bring.

Just then the door went silent as its larger door was unlocked from the inside and opened. The girl was gently pulled aside by one of her older brothers to allow for the funeral congregation to pass.

The grandfather's body, covered in a white shroud, was carried on a wooden stretcher. Its planks smoothly passed from shoulder to shoulder.

As the crowd carried the body away, the girl stood in the middle of the now fully open larger door.

When the crowd disappeared into the distance, the door spoke again.

"I am also a door that was built for death. My width was specifically designed to allow the maximum number of people to share in the blessings of helping carry a body away to be returned to the earth it came from.

I am a door of life, death, war and peace.
Such were the intentions of the hands that carved me.
I am a door for all seasons.

I am a door ready for all."

The girl looked up at the door with her
now smothered mascaraed eyes and
said

"Well they sure don't make them like
you anymore."

Tears Of A Mountain

There was once a poet who wished to
become the greatest poet in the world.
He practiced writing his poems all day
and all night.

Won the admirations of many and
became a living legend. Still he was
not convinced he was the greatest poet
of them all.

Not until I can make a mountain cry
with my poetry will I see myself as the
best. Moving a mountain to tears is a
worthy challenge for some one such as
I.

And so the poet began to compose his
masterpiece, the poem that would at
last accomplish his every waking
moment's dream.
To be the greatest poet this world had
ever seen.

He vanished from people's sight for the longest time. Many thought he had died or simply gone insane.
But then he appeared again.

I have written a poem that is to move a mountain to tears, and tomorrow I shall set forth up to the mountains to claim my prize.

The poet climbed the mountain nearby and found himself in the middle of an empty valley chiseled by water far long gone.

He stood on top of a flat rock and began to read to the mountain his masterpiece.

When the poet was, done nothing occurred.

The poet's efforts had all been in vain.

But just before he was to set back to his village, he heard a loud explosion from the earth.

A dormant spring erupted back into life. As water trickled out from the mountain's heart, clouds carrying much needed rain began to cluster above. Rain fell with an intensity it had not done before.

The poet was so joyful that he had at last accomplished his task that he did not see the flood approaching.

The poet was swept away, never to be seen again, by the tears he had evoked from the mountain and the sky.

Daawa

Daawa is not about knocking on a person's door and trying to spark off a religious debate.

It's not about winning an argument or proving a point.

Daawa to me is about being a shining example to others through your actions.

It's about behaving in an inspiring way that invites people to reflect internally about their own position. By so doing, kick-start the wheels of spiritual consciousness deep within them.

What good are your sermons when they see that the Justice you preach was absent when you left the water at

home running in such a wasteful
manner?

What good are your books about
Peace, when they hear you swear and
curse in traffic jams and drive like you
alone own the road?

What good do your colour pamphlets
do you when the Equality To All,
which is printed on them, is thrown out
of the window when you reject your
daughter's suitor for merely being
from another tribe?

Actions speak louder than words, my
friend.
Daawa is not about knocking on
people's doors.
It's about living a life that invites
others to come and knock on yours.

Fruits Of The Heart

Understanding is the function of the
human heart.
It is the very tool that determines how far
the truth and we are apart.

Love and hate are like two competing
plants that grow on the land of our hearts.
Hate is a weed that grows rapidly if left
unchecked. A heart full of hate cannot
carry out its proper function. As a result,
ignorance reigns free.
Now I know it's a dull day's work and, at
the best of times, such a chore, but we
must weed out our hearts' soil every day.
Then into our hearts the seed of love we
must sow.
Then and only then can we expect the fruit
of understanding to grow.

Unfortunately, most of us lack the
discipline required to keep our hearts
clean. Love-deprived hearts are paranoid
creatures, and tend to blame their life's
misfortunes on everything under the sun

92

apart from themselves. They blame the
Jews, Zionists, Arabs, Muslims, Hindus,
Sikhs, Christians, Sunnas, Shias,
Protestants, Catholics, Dutch, the Blacks,
some famous singer or movie star who
does a sexy scene.
Some of them even blame the Mother
Queen (bless her cotton socks).

The struggle between love and hate for the
domination of the human heart is as old as
time. The word struggle in Arabic is Jihd,
which is the origin of the word Jihad.
There are two types of Jihad. The greater
Jihad, which is the struggle of love and
hate in the heart, and the lesser Jihad,
where outside the body the struggle starts.

Weed-infested hearts lack understanding,
and so they confuse the lesser war for the
greater. They mistake the shadows for the
true forms, as my good friend Plato would
have said. To regain understanding, one
must get rid of the entire weed
surrounding the heart, and once that's
done, it must be maintained. The trick is to

do a little bit a day so nothing is piled. It's
sort of like keeping all your paper work in
the office filed.

Do you know who introduced me to the
true meaning of Jihad? For even I thought
it just meant war. It was a German Taoist,
would you believe? The Taoist had
reached a stage in his heart's development
that allowed him to eat from the fruits of
understanding.

Through his words alone I came to
understand the true meaning of the word
Islam. Islam means peace. That many of
us know, but what type of peace does the
word refer to? The kind you want before
you take a book to read?
Or the type you seek, when sleep is what
you need?

Islam is the peace your heart needs for
love to grow. It's a condition of your
heart's soil. A Muslim to me is a person
who eats from the fruit of understanding.
All people who eat from this fruit are

Muslims, no matter what they call their
religion or belief system.
So you see, who better to teach me about
Islam than my Taoist friend? Likewise,
all who have weed-infested hearts are far
away from being Muslim, no matter what
they call themselves, even if it's Islam.
For Islam is not something you can jump
in and out of like a cart. It's much deeper
than that, it's a condition of the human
heart.

A Pilot's Prayers

Why can't you stay home on Thursday
like all the other dads do?
Why do you have to go and fly your
small plane?
What would happen to us if you
crashed and died?
I would have no father then!
The little girl complained to her sports
pilot dad.

Don't cry, little one.
If I crash, then it is God's will that
death meet me in the sky.
Death, dear child, comes to us
wherever we are.

If I do crash, then be sure to tell your
mother to have them bury me a martyr,
Smiled the sports pilot dad.

What's a Martyr?

It's a person who dies whilst pursuing
to be a better human being.
When I fly up there, over the clouds, I
become a better person. A better dad,
A person who is anything but sad.

A Visiting Flower

When a person you know is taken ill,
it is the duty of the true friend to visit
them. Even if the visit feels a bit
awkward, it must be done.

It must be pushed up your priority list
of the day.
For these visits carry many blessings.

There is a blessing for the ill person.
Their souls get uplifted, knowing that
there are a few in their lives that truly
care about them even when they have
nothing of benefit to offer them in
return.

There are blessings for the visitor in
two kinds. Firstly, they get to
appreciate their own state of well
being, and so use it more wisely.
Secondly, they get to plant a seed for

their own souls to be uplifted one day.
Possibly on a day they need it most.

Your visit to the ill must be kept short,
like this poem, for you do not wish to
burden the ill in any way.

Speak only of positive things and
make sure you smile a lot. In many
cultures, flowers do the job. But in
mine, the visiting human is the flower.

Why 7 Not 5?

Why do we go round the Kabba 7
times, why not 5?
Asked the young lady to the Imam.

The Imam replied,

The truth is we don't truly know why.
We were told to do so by our beloved
Prophet and our devotion to him is
such that we entrust our lives to his
teachings.

That is not to say we follow with out
reason.

Reason plays a key role in accepting
Islam. Faith on the other hand plays a
key role in being able to follow it.

Remember, my daughter, that Islam is
about your whole life which spans this
world and the next.

Going round the Kabba 7 times and
not more or less will have a benefit to
us not in this life but the next.

The next life is where all things are
clear.

The Holy Qoran says,
'Thou was heedless of this, now have
we removed thy veil, And sharp is thy
sight **This Day**' 50:22

Plato called it the world of true forms.
A world where everything appears as it
truly is.

Your question reminds me of a story.

One day, Imam Jaffar Al Sadiq (AS)
sat resting by the Kabba as the
pilgrims did their Tawaf.

A man approached him and mockingly asked:
Till when will you people keep splitting and grinding seeds?

He was trying to indicate that the Tawaf around the Kabba was nothing more than the equivalent of a mill moved by a donkey. Thus saying Islam was a waste of time.

The Imam looked at him with patient eyes and replied,

If we are wrong and you are right, then we have lost very little.
But if we are right and you are wrong, then you would have lost it all.

Silent Thoughts

"Music is Haram
It is a tool the Shaitan used to sway
mankind from the righteous path,"
Said the man to the crowd that filled
the rectangular Arabian Majlis.

None said a word in return, for this
was not a two-way conversation but a
sermon. But there sat somewhere
in the audience a soul whose silent
thoughts begged to differ with what
was being said. The soul's silent
thoughts spoke thus:

*Does the call to prayer not have
harmony?
Does not the Talbiya at Haj carry a
tune?
Do you think the likes of Abdel Baset
Abdel Sammad and Khalil Al Hussany
are strangers to rhythm?
Music is found all over Islam.*

For how could it not be so?

In the golden days of Islamic intellectual development, days that have sadly (very sadly) gone, music was studied by all Islamic scholars as a branch of mathematics, philosophy and medicine.

Our history books all state that the likes of Al Kindi, Al Farabi, Ibn Sina and Al Ghazali all wrote books on music and its benefits in healing bodies and purifying souls. Are these intellectual giants all going to hell? Are they also tools of the Shaitan?

Today we live in a Muslim world where saying such thoughts out loud would be impossible.
But having them in your silent mind is fine.

Sunna / Shia

Was it supposed to go to Imam Ali or
another?
Do you fold your hands when you pray
or keep them straight?
Do you prostrate on earth or carpet?
Is marriage only permanent or can it
be temporary?

Sunna this, Shia that,
Arguing amongst each other whilst
your enemies grow fat.

They grow fat off your self-made
division.
They grow stronger as you make your
separate decisions.

I find those who dwell on such matters
to be of the type that would argue their
point over and above that of the sound
of the Muathin's call, knowing not that
they had done so at all.

Let each live their life, so long as they
don't prevent you from doing the
same.
Tolerance after all is Islam's main
game.

For every good Shia there is a good
Sunni.
The same goes for their bad and ugly.

Learn to play the game of Islam.
Muslims, no matter what sect, are all
the same.

The Sound Of Music

Some say Music is simply sound.
This means that the rustling of the
leaves and the sound of the ocean
meeting the shore are all brilliant
symphonies composed by God, the
greatest composer of all.

Others say Music is not just any sound
but sound that is organized by man
into harmony and melody.
This in turn means that's music is
nothing more than an extension of the
human soul.
Souls can either be good or bad and
therefore whatever extended from
these souls, be it music or other wise,
also follows suit.

Good music to me is that which
touches my soul in a way that makes
me a better human, it helps distribute

love, compassion, positive creativity
and healing.

Bad music also touches my soul but in
a way that makes me less of a human.
It spreads in me anger, hate, the selfish
pursuit of thoughtless lust and greed.

I think it was best said by Mozart,
possibly the greatest human composer
the world has ever seen:

"Music is not in the notes, but in the
pause between."

Scotland

Where it rains all the time but the people
always shine.
No storm can beat them, no loss put them
down.
Scotland, land of my birth, land of the
truly brave.

I was born in Edinburgh, in the Royal
Infirmary, to be exact.
Went to the best schools, wore the best
uniforms, and was brought up to be a
nobleman.
I spent my wee years as a toddler there,
and soon I began to grow, but Dubai
wanted me back, so that my forefathers'
origins would not go.

But destiny
had me return to the land of my birth.
This time Glasgow would be called my
turf.
As a young, gullible, overseas university
student, Glasgow found me looking all
proper, posh and prime.

109

It shook its head at me and said,

*"We is gonna av to toughenz u up, sunny
Jim."*

And so it did.
Glasgow taught me how to be a man, how
to love, how to fight, and how finding
freedom in the mists of slavery is the
focus of every warrior's sight.

And so my Scottish education is now
complete. A noble warrior is what it made
me.

The Arabs and the Scots have much in
common, didn't you know? Don't believe
me? Well come then, and let me help you
see.

We both wear skirts with very little
underneath. We will both fight you till the
bitter end, and no, we are not afraid to use
our teeth.

We love football and have a few historic issues with the English. Oh and ai, we both have weird parts of animals as our national dishes.

We are people of the clan, the Scots and us, where the collective benefit of all rises above that of any one man. We love to see our falcons fly, with legendary poets always nearby.

We have more than our fair share of famous inventors, from whose work many a great human accomplishment was stirred.
And in both our lands the sound of the mystical bagpipes can be heard.

In me, an Arabian Scot is what you see, proud of both parts of me I am. Ai, proud of both parts of me, I will always be. For an Arabian Scot is what you will always see, in me.

Khaleeji

I am the son of the Daffa.
Its soft blackness protected and
nurtured me.
I am the son of the wooden Dows with
their curved triangular sail that carried
Pearl Divers out to the sea.

I am the son of the palm trees that
gave us food, shelter and shaded us
from the sun.
I am the son of the desert ships whose
existence carried blessings that were
second to none.

I am the son of the Bakour, elaborately
decorated Hennaed hands and rose
water sprinklers.
I am the son of the joyous news these
things bring.
Ululating sounds that make the soul
sing.

I am the son of the desert, with its shifting sands that remind us that nothing stays the same except the mercy of God and his glory.

I am the son of the amazing people who live in these magical lands.

I am the son of those who are a living proof that man can bring life to anywhere thought dead.
I am the son of their struggle for life, their poetry-filled nights and their many love stories.

I am the son of the Baharana and their Hussaini tears that wash away sin.
I am the son of the Ajam and their Barjeers that soothed our sun-baked skin.

I am the son of the Balutch and their brightly coloured clothes, I am the son

of the Arab Bedu with their greetings
with the nose.

I am the son of those who brought
music into our lives, I am the son of
the African tribes.

I am the son of the Arabian Gulf, or as
we say, the Khaleej,
I am a product of its very soil.
I am the son of a land that has so much
more to offer the world
than just oil.

Cape Town

Cape Town is the city of my poetic birth.
Why? I have no idea, but no one chooses
   his birthplace, it is chosen for them.

It's earth spoke to me as soon as I arrived
and said, *"Your people have the freedom
our people fought so hard for; yet you do
   not appreciate it. You bask and bathe
under freedom's sun, knowing not its true
   glory. There are a few chapters missing
that you have not read; when it comes to
    the novel of freedom's story.*

*Here, my child, take with you in your
  heart a gift from me to you. Take the
benefit of hundreds of years of pain and
suffering and use it to remind your people
    of the true value of freedom.
For only on the foundation of freedom can
   you build a truly just kingdom."*

"But I am not worthy of this gift, dear
      earth that speaks,

your own children are more worthy than
me."

*"My own children are focused on healing
the wounds from within, they have enough
work to do, believe me.
It is for my children's sake that I ask you
to help them.
It is a request, not an order, so what say
you, desert child?"*

"I accept! But why me?"

*"For two reasons, one is the condition of
your heart, which we see as a good ally.
The other is your distance from us. You
see, sometimes you can only feel things
from afar. Take the constant roar of the
ocean, you can't hear it from the sands of
the beach where you are so near to it, but
you can from up in the mountains where
you are far.*

*Now you must go, desert child, for I have
much repair to do. Use the centuries of*

our struggle, the blood and pain, and use
it as the wind in your Arabian sail.
Do that, and you will not fail."

Ramadan

Thank you, oh most holy month of the
year.
Oh you, who was chosen to give the very
best gift to this sphere.

Honoured above the other eleven you are.
Separated from the rest like a shining star.

In you, the final Prophet (PBUH) was told
to "Read". In you, the Quran planted its
first seed.

Brought down to all humanity, and not the
Arabs alone. In you, life can be given even
to a stone.

The last ten days of Ramadan are when
these miracles occurred. The last ten days
of Ramadan is when this poet's poems
were cooked and stirred.

It was then, on every night of these last ten
days, I asked your creator and mine to
help me make my heart pure. To make

my heart speak to other hearts, about what
best method there is to cure.

That's when the poems started to roll, or
should I say, erupt. For nothing could stop
them, not even sleep.

Thank you for being so kind. I hope I am
worthy of this gift.
And the day I am not, is the day it should
go adrift.

Cape Malay

They came from the East as slaves in
captivity.
Their freedom foundations were already
set, and so the slave trade did not affect
their mentality.

Stripped of their royal rights they carried
with them only two. The caramel skin on
their backs and the Islam that their hearts
knew.

They were carried to a land that said black
was not the same as white, and all those
who thought otherwise would be banished
from sight.

And so the lions of the East accepted the
challenge, and fought the evil rule on two
fronts. The physical, which claimed many
martyrs, and the spiritual, by preaching
equality in secret, up in the mountains
where many of their graves are still found.
Up in the mountain where their essence is
still bound.

They were murdered and tortured for the privilege of prostrating to a Lord that said, "All mankind is one, and that love, knowledge and integrity belong to every human under the sun."

For three hundred years they fought alongside others for the freedom of the human soul. For three hundred years they fought alongside others to see the freedom flag flap from that pole.

As Allah Almighty is my witness, I see the Cape Malays to be far better Muslims than us Arabs. They may not understand each word found in the holy verses, but they live and breathe them. We Arabs may understand but we fail to act. Now, I ask you honestly, what good to humanity is that?

Now to get the best of both worlds is always a good thing. A Muslim who understands and acts is made of the same material as the Islamic legends of old. The

best humanity has ever seen, that is why
this Arab chose to marry a Cape Malay
Queen.

Why Do You Love Me?

Why do you love me?
Asks my wife from time to time

My answer is always the same.

Never ask why you are loved.
It's like asking me why does the moon
look so beautiful?

Such things don't require a why?
Instead they should be used to help
you spread your wings and fly.

Fly to a place where you can truly be
you, and in so doing spread the
maximum amount of goodness to the
world.

For, if you are not you, then the
amount of goodness you do manage to
spread will only be a fraction of your
potential.

Love is the wind beneath our wings.

Your love for me has taken me to the
world of poetry.
It is there I now soar and glide.

So don't ask me why I love you.
Instead, use my love to spread your
wings and fly.

Wedding Ring

An abandoned wedding ring lies beside
me. My wife's words from last night still
in my ears.
"I no longer wish to be married to you;
and, here, take back your stupid ring."
Why do loved ones' angry words always
manage to sting?

Although she has done this to me before,
this time feels different. This time, I really
feel like I will not get up after this fall.
Perhaps I should replace this ring with a
ping-pong ball.

For this episode has gone to and fro
countless number of times. Which makes
me think, why do we need a ring? Why
does our marriage have to be represented
by such a thing? Who came up with the
idea of a wedding ring anyway? I wonder
what the history books have to say.

Rooted in paganism, orientated in a time when idolatry was in fashion, no wonder I never took to it with a passion.

Anyway, so there I am looking down at this pagan thing, when a friend calls me and invites me to take part in an adventure. We are to climb a mountain. A mountain called Lion's Head.

"Lion's Head? I don't know, dude. Sounds rather fierce."

"You'll be fine; it's an easy climb. Besides, your prize will be a life-altering view of the city. Not doing it whilst you are here would be such a sin."

"Life-altering did you say? Hmm, not doing it a sin?
Alright then, I'm in."

We pass by the most beautiful scenery on the way to the top. Beautiful green plants, isles of yellow flowers, the sounds of beetles humming, Muslim graves, dark

caves chiseled with the great signature of
time.

The last few steps of climbing a mountain
are always the most challenging. It's when
you ask yourself, "Is this really what I
seek? But I can't stop now, for I am too
close to the peak."
The view from up there is indeed life-
altering. You can see all of the city from
this small platform. The generosity this
small space gives us is immense. Just like
poetry.
You get given so much from so little.
Poetry to me is the very definition of
efficiency.

An endless blue ocean is now staring me
in the face, saying to me, "This is how
much you should dream." I close my eyes
and let the sound of the roaring ocean fill
my ears, and the cold mountain breeze
brush my face. I open my eyes and know
what I have to do. I take out my
abandoned wedding ring, this pagan thing,
and with all my might I cast it into the

endless blue sky. I watch it float into endless dream, and watch it being carried away by eternity's stream.

We rest a while, and have something to eat. You must always admire the view to the maximum whilst sitting on any mountain peak. Time waits for no man, not even a mountain for that matter. Now we must now head back. Many poems were captured this day, all put into my poet's sack.

Something very strange occurred on the way down. But to those of you who think like me, this situation will not be as strange as it sounds.

First two butterflies came out of nowhere and greeted me. Then birds of all sorts hovered above me, gliding effortlessly over the deep blue sea. As I passed the isle of yellow flowers, which now turned into solid gold, the sound of ululating beetles filled my soul. The green plants, which I had passed earlier, now reflect silver from their leaves. Then I smelt the perfume of incense that came from the Muslim graves. Everything seemed to be filled with light, even the darkest caves.

Gold, silver, ululating and incense put together can only mean one thing. The mountain had accepted my ring.

Now marrying a mountain has got to be the strangest thing I have done in my life. My only worry now is: how am I to explain this to my wife?

Mum, How Are You?

You bathed me in nothing but love. You
fed me nothing but compassion. You
brought me up to be a star model in good
manners' fashion.

Your aristocratic blood runs through my
veins. Your people's humility, the same.
You left your island paradise and came to
live in what was then a desolate land. As
an ambassador of life, you tried to plant
love into their desert sands. But despite
your efforts, nothing grew. For the people
were set in their ways and did not like
anything new.

So wisely you gave all your love to your
children, and their love grew. Love grew
to be a tall mighty palm tree, Mum. A tree
that will always shade and feed you no
matter what. For you did the same to us
when we were in the cot.

How could we forget all that you have
done and endured, all for the sake of
seeing us from society's ill cured?

You gave us the best birthdays every year,
even when your pay cheque was nowhere
near.
You knitted us big warm woolly jumpers
when we studied abroad,
and taught us that reading was the best
cure for being bored.

You bought us the Guinness Book of
World Records every year, to tell us we
should not only keep up, but should set the
pace for our peers.

No poem could ever capture your love for
us, or our love for you, but here are just a
few things I, your eldest son, would like to
say to you.

You're a Libran mum, just like me,
and I am truly proud to be part of your
family tree.

You were open-minded enough to accept
my chosen life, despite what the crowd
told you. You stood by me when no one
did and said, son, do what you must do
with no fear, for your mother loves you.

Now I might have grown up, Mum, even
have a few grey hairs, but I will always be
your first-born, and you will always be my
Mum.
The one that bathed me in nothing but
love and fed me nothing but compassion,
the one that brought me up to be a model
in good manners' fashion. I only want to
make you proud, Mum. Do good things
that make you shout with joy, "That's my
boy."

Now saying, "Mum how are you?" to
your mother is never enough. Whenever I
visit my Mum, this is what I do. I greet her
with a huge smile, I kiss her honoured
forehead, and then I look her in the eyes
and say, "Mum, how are you?"

If you are lucky enough to have a mum
like mine then this is what you should do,
it's more worthy than just saying the
words, "Mum how are you?"

World Leader

Can you imagine the leader of your country driving their own car, stuck in traffic with the rest of you? I can with mine, for now.

Can you imagine your leader walking alone on the public streets with no body guards or cameras as they take a stroll to have a good think? I can with mine, for now.

Can you image your leader writing a book of poems that speaks of their dreams, their love and personal aspirations? I can with mine, for now.

But alas, what my leader does and doesn't do is of no worth to you, for you are the World Leaders today. Its up to you to lead and us to follow isn't that correct? Well if that's the case one begs to ask, where exactly are you leading us to?

Sibling Rivalry

Curly Hair, Tender Butterfly, Swift
Deer and Shining Star are my siblings.
Rare diamonds and jewels they are,
Born from love.
A step ahead of the rest by far.

They made history in our tribe even
before they turned eighteen.
They have gone much further than I
would have ever dreamed.

They have reached the deepest oceans,
conquered the highest hills and
outwitted the most dangerous of
wolves and serpents.

Many in the tribe often ask me about
why I too did not turn out to be so
special, did the blessings perhaps miss
a generation?

I reply with a smile, forgiving them of
their ignorance; for they might have
not been reared out of love like us.
In our tent, our accomplishments are
like a peace pipe smoked by the elders.
It is one, it is shared.

Although true, I am not the smartest of
them by any means. But
as the eldest, it is my duty not to be the
smartest, but to pave the way, to draw
the maps of un-charted lands and seas
and point them to where potholes and
traps may lie.
The battle wounds that cover my body
and heart are medals of Honour. Not
just for me alone but for my siblings as
well.

As a big brother, I watch over them
with great pride from my perch.
Although they are now spread all over
the great plains of this earth, they must

know that I am only a Golden Eagle's
distance away.
If ever support were needed in battle,
all they would have to do is call, and I
would be there at once, Tomahawk in
one hand and shield in the other.

To my siblings' adversaries, I say only
this. Any of you who try and hurt my
siblings in any way will have to
answer me. When I hunt and track you
down, trust me, the wisest thing for
you to do is run for cover.
For here I am, Soaring Eagle, known
to my siblings as
Big Brother.

Me And My Rasta Hat

I walk around town wearing my Rasta hat.
My friend David Marshal calls it a tea
cosy,
But that's just him being a bit cheeky and
nosy.

But I'll have you all know that my
beloved mother knitted the hat for me. So
this Rasta hat is very special. It's also
made in the UAE.

I know it looks pretty weird, especially
when I wear it with my Kandoorah, but
it's still me under that hat, not some dude
from Bora Bora.

Now my Rasta hat has functions. I'm
telling you it's no simple thing, it makes
others smile, especially kids. I guess it's
because I look like a man with a colourful
mushroom on his head.

It helps me net my thoughts, keep them
close to my head, else I forget them
instead.

It also gives me that bohemian look. I kid
you not, when I say that without my Rasta
hat, I might have not been able to finish
this book.

Now since we are on the subject of Rasta,
we might as well go all the way. Now
opinions are divided on the matter, but this
is what I have to say.

Rasta is not all smoke, you know. That's
what shallow people only see. Rasta is like
all things in life. It's what you wish it to
be. I love Reggae music, especially Bob
Marley and Peter Tosh.

These gentlemen, when it comes to history
and self-identity, have a lot to say. Their
music carries a serious message, but
passed to you in a kind-hearted way.

I love the Rasta colours. They just make
me smile. The black, green and the yellow
inspire me to be a jolly fellow.

I love the concept behind the I and I.
Where the first I represents the individual,
the other I is their place in humanity.

So before this poem ends, allow me to say
farewell in a Rasta way, by saying, I and I
bid you all *One Love* and *Equal Rights*.
Yah mon, that is all this Rasta Arab has to
say.

Against All Odds

So you think you can't do it.
You're too young, too old, too
inexperienced, too weak, too dumb.
And about a million other excuses you can
use, and then still make up some.

Truth be told, you have reasons to be
concerned, for the odds of success are
truly against you, this is a statistic fact.
Haven't you heard of the 90-10 rule? A
man called Robert Kiyosaki introduced
me to the idea.
All in a wonderful book called "Rich
Dad, Poor Dad" suggested to me by a
peer.

According to this rule, financial success is
a minority's game. It states that only 10%
of all those who desire to be rich will
actually become rich.

The rest remain in normality's ditch. The
same odds can be applied to successful
movie stars, singers, dancers, writers,

painters, athletes and newly established businesses, to name a few.

So to all of you with a dream, a dream to make it big, I figure your chances of failure are also about 90%. You try getting a bank loan with that, "Yes, can I get a loan for a project that has a 90% chance of failure, please?"

The bank manager will probably just look at you very strangely, knowing not how to reply. It's then you should say the following:

Dear Manager, I know a 90% failure rate sounds pretty bad, but just give me five minutes of your time, and I'm sure you'll look back at this situation being very glad.

You see, I have beaten these odds before, and so have you, I might add.
It's just we humans tend to forget the good things that happen to us, and that, dear Manager, is what is truly sad.

I, Mr. Manager, stand as living proof, for I am one in a hundred million chance. Out of a hundred million sperm, I was the one that made it through; I am one of the biggest odd busters this universe ever knew.

If I could make it against those odds once, I know I can do it again. My will power and belief in my dream can beat any odds. I was born out of the very notion, so why not give me the financial means to acquire my magic potion.

Trust me, your bank will not look at this as an experience that is sore.
You can relax, dear Manager, for I have beaten bigger odds before.

Going To The Movies

I love the movies, don't you? I just love
watching all those stars.
They take me out of this world, and make
me feel like I'm living on Mars.
I don't know about you, but I always go
extra early to pick the best seats, I make
sure that my position allows the audio
system to give me a kiss-ass beat.

I purchase my ticket and go chill in the
café. I look into the crowd and see such a
varied lot. Men, women and children of all
ages, the story of their lives written on
their faces. I read a few pages, whist I sit,
wondering how a guy like that ended up
with a girl so fit.

When take off is near, I head for the door,
can't miss the trailers, life without them
would be such a bore. Now in the theater I
sit waiting for the movie to begin.

My popcorn nice and warm, and my water
bottle next to me. Glad I'm not sitting
behind that tall fellow, for I'd never be
able to see.
When the movie begins, I study each part
attentively like my life depends on it. How
could you not do the same? If I didn't, I
would forever walk in shame. A movie is
a piece of art, you see, and I love art. Me
and she are never far apart.

But do you know what the best movies
are? Even better than the ones with all the
stars? It is the ones you can hold in your
hands. The ones that put you in
Spielberg's seat.
Now, wouldn't that be a fancy treat? In a
book, when you read the words "*in walked
a gorgeous lady,*" it's up to you to create
her, put your imagination to work, shake it
up, and give it a stir. In my director's
mind, I see tanned skin, long wavy black
hair, big hazel eyes and a hipster lycra
skirt that embraces her thighs. I see the
kind of girl that would make busy traffic

stop, the kind of girl that would make your
eyes pop.

Now directing your own movie through
reading a book is cool.
But writing your own script is a rare
jewel. So having said that, let me ask you
a question, If you were a movie that all
went to see, what kind of movie would
you be?

A horror, a comedy, or thriller perhaps?
Would you make people laugh or would
you make them cry? Would you be deep
or would you be shallow? Would you be a
short film, or long one? Black & white, or
colour? Would you have a sad ending or a
live-happily-ever-after one?

Me, I think I would be a Kung Fu movie.
I'd be the hero, of course, and I'd kick
some serious ass, but I would not kill
anyone. I would be a Kung Fu Master,
warrior of the good. I'd love my enemies
and show them the way to think about

where their life in this ever-expanding
universe stood.

I'd defeat the main villain, and the true
whereabouts of my kidnapped heroin, I
would make him blurt. I'd rescue her, and
she would be none other than the one in
the hipster lycra skirt.

The movie would end and I would die
fighting for a good cause. You would
stand up at the end and give me a grand
applause.

By the time you leave the theatre, I'd still
be with you. I would have made you laugh
from your heart, and cry from there too.
I'd make you think and ponder about what
lies over yonder.

You'd buy me as a DVD and put me on
whenever you needed a lift. I'd also make
an ideal birthday gift.

Yup, I think that would be me. Me as I'd
like to be seen by the world.

Direct your own movie, be your own star.
Live your movie for real, that to me is a
really big deal.

Flight

I love watching birds fly;
With their wings spread wide, they
glide effortless in the sky.

They are not bound by any earthly
limitations whilst airborne. Released
from the shackles of gravity, they take
to their true ingenious design.

But getting airborne is the most
demanding part of a bird's flight.
Take off is no easy thing.

Some birds achieve take off by using
their strong legs to leap into the air
then flapping their wings downwards;
others like the Albatross have to taxi
along a flat surface like a plane.
They run run run run run run until the
air flowing over their wings lifts them
up into the heavens.

Smaller birds with less muscle power simply throw themselves off a high platform and glide themselves into flight.

Human dreams are creatures of flight too.

When airborne, human dreams seem effortless to the onlooker. But it's a result of much sacrifice, hard work, dedication and perseverance.

All our dreams are born with wings, We are all born with the tools for flight.

Putting the tools to their proper use is always going to be our biggest fight.

But once we achieve lift off, even if it's just for a second, we'll know we are on the right track.
We must keep trying and trying.

The second will become one and a half, then two, three, four, and before we know it, we'll lose count all together.

For now we are flying in the sky. Our earthly gravitational worries now nowhere nearby.

We just need to master take off once, just once. And as I am sure any bird of flight will tell us,
The rewards of flight far exceed the efforts exerted at take off.

Grounded dreams are indeed a sorry sight, and perhaps the number one reason why many humans are so unhappy.

So for the sake of humanity, learn to fly.
It's a mission to put your design as a human being to a purpose that is true.

Don't forget, human dreams are
creatures of flight too.

WD-40

WD-40 is quite an amazing thing.
It's multipurpose galores.
Cleans, protects, loosens rusty parts,
stops squeaks and does much, much
more.

Wish I had a WD-40 to sort out all the
many squeaks in my life.
Something I could magically spray
over me to help clean my soul and
loosen the rusty parts that prevent me
from accomplishing my dreams.

Wonder what formula such a spray
would use?
Love mixed with faith, hope, positivity
and self-belief perhaps?

I think we all have the ability to make
our own personal WD-40 spray.
Something that we always keep
nearby. Something that is as

multipurpose as a pocket Swiss Army knife.
For there truly is nothing worse than a jammed or rusted life.

Dance With Failure

Learn to dance with failure, my friend,
only then love she will send.
When you have won over failure's heart,
only then will true success invite you to
play a part.

In school we were taught, we must
succeed, succeed and succeed,
"That's very good sir, but what about its
seed?"

"Never mind the seed, laddi.
Who has the time for that? You must win,
win win,
even if it means throwing your conscience
in the bin."

In school they take away a mark when you
make a mistake.
But life is not like that.
In life a mistake is the best thing you can
make.

The first thing an Aikidoka learns to do is
to fall.
Only then will they hear the honorable
warrior in them call.
They start their mission with the art of
what we call making a mistake.
There is much wisdom in that for all to
take.

Take this poem as another example.
Do you know how many drafts I had to
go through to make these words worthy of
your eyes?
I had to go through many failures, and not
one of them do I look at with despise.
They were simply the stepping stones I
took towards you.

Yes, Mr. Poet. We understand the thought.
But how does it translate into action?
You must admit, failure is not pretty; she
tastes bitter and kinda stinks.
Most of us avoid her like she's some sort
of jinx.

The first thing you have to do is get the
idea of winning and losing out of your
head.
Take them both and kick them out of bed.
Now when they're well and truly gone,
you should feel more relaxed. Like getting
all your income without worrying about
the tax.

Then in this new-found state of peace, I
need you to follow this poet's golden
motto:
Do it in the dark and repeat, repeat, repeat.

Doing something in the dark is like doing
it when no one is looking.
When no one is looking, you don't care
how many times you mess up, right?
Failure in the dark is no big deal. So close
your eyes and pretend no one is there.
For only when you are in the dark will
you find your spark.

Now, once you've got that spark, it's just
a question of repetition.

Endless repetition. For repetition is the
key to all the great legends you see.

I have danced with failure so many times.
I have danced the Salsa, the Twist , the
Waltz and even done the bump and grind,
but true love, she helped me find.

Show me a person who always wins and
I'll show you the biggest loser of them all.

Learn to dance with failure, my friend,
only then love she will send.
When you have won over failure's heart,
only then will true success invite you to
play a part.

Love What You Do, Love You

Khalil Gibran once said, "Work is love
made visible."
Now, me, I'm nowhere near as deep as the
big K, but here is what I have to say:

You must love what you do.
Loving what you do must be the greatest
love you ever knew. You must be at one
with what you do. You must live it, breath
it, eat it and drink it too.
You must see what you do all around
you. It must be the first thing you think of
when you wake up, and the last thought
before you go to sleep. When it comes to
your love, you must never fear falling in
too deep.

When you work without being time-
bound,
then, my friend, it is love you have found.

When work is fun, half the work is done,
or so they say. But to me, it is more like

when work is fun, there is no work any
more, it is just done.

Love what you do. Love your job, love
your hobby, love your wife.
In short, love your life.

A Poem To Myself

Well Wael, you got your first book of
poems. Was it all worth it? Is the glory
worth the pain?

Yes, it sure is, my man, for it kept me
sane.

How do you feel now, you have
accomplished what you set out to do?

Like a man who has just risked everything
to climb a mountain. I am now sitting at
the peak overlooking this magnificent
view. Sitting from up here like a Golden
Eagle, I can see all the valleys and rivers I
have had to cross. Boy, what a journey! I
had so much fun, but I must say the
mountain over there does look a little
higher than the one I am on.

But for now, I am very content with this
view. As Allah Almighty is my witness,
it's the greatest view this poet's eyes ever
knew.

The End

Glossary of Arabic Terminology

Kandoorah: *UAE national dress*
Emarati: *A UAE National*
Abra: *Small boat*
Abbar: *Boats men*
Daawa: *Preaching*
Kabba: *Cube Shaped structure found in Mecca, Saudi Arabia. Direction in which all Muslims pray*
Imam: *Muslim Religious Person*
Tawaf: *Circumambulation of the Kabba*
Haram: *Forbidden*
Shaitan: *Devil*
Mijils: *Arabic living room*
Talbiya: *Chant*
Haj: *Islamic pilgrimage*
Khaleeji: *A native of the Arabian/Persian Gulf*
Daffa: *Black over coat worn by women*
Bakour: *Incense*
Baharana: *A Gulf Arab Shia*
Ajam: *A person of Persian origin*
Balutch: *A person with Balutchistani origins*

164

Ramadan: 9th Islamic month of the year where fasting is obligatory

*Ramadan: 9th Islamic month of the year
where fasting is obligatory*